KENTUCKY

A Picture Book to Remember Her by

CRESCENT BOOKS
NEW YORK

Featuring the Photography of Andrew Heaps
CLB 861
© 1986 Illustrations and text: Colour Library Books Ltd.,
   Guildford, Surrey, England.
Text filmsetting by Acesetters Ltd., Richmond, Surrey, England.
1986 edition published by Crescent Books, distributed by Crown Publishers, Inc.
Printed in Spain.
ISBN 0 517 47803 X
h g f e d c b a

Kentucky is usually regarded as the land of Colonel Sanders and Jack Daniel, of the Kentucky Derby and endless miles of bluegrass. It is also poverty-stricken Appalachia, often provincial and isolated.

Daniel Boone was the first to hack away at the isolation when he began exploring the territory in the mid-18th century. Right through the turn of the century, it was considered the Wild West and thousands moved there anxious to tame it. By the time it was made a state in 1792, it was home to more people than most others. But the same spirit that lured them there in the first place encouraged then to move even further westward as new territories opened up. Among the men who felt the tug was Tom Lincoln, who took his young son Abraham and his wife Nancy west to Indiana and then to Illinois.

Kentucky was neutral in the Civil War, but eventually threw in its lot with the Union. But before that happened, it had sent its sons to fight on both sides. The result was that when the fighting was officially over, blood feuds began in the hills of Kentucky that lasted for generations.

Fighting among themselves in a different way is a point of pride and a long-standing tradition among Kentuckians. Since the day they sent Henry Clay to the United States Senate, they have been crazy about politics and great stump speakers are among the most famous men in the state's history. The politicians play by one rule that makes winning everything. They'll promise you anything, tell you whatever you want to hear. And their constituents love them for it.

On the other hand, once a man has won, then he has a job to do. One former Governor once told an interviewer that there were only two things in life to be avoided: gonorrhea and being Governor of Kentucky. The problem is that as much as Kentuckians enjoy a good political speech, they enjoy the right to go to the public servants for help of all sorts, from getting a road paved to giving their son a little push to get him out of high school. The result is that one shrewd governor generations ago began getting around unreasonable requests by giving away the title of Colonel to what might otherwise have become a disappointed citizen. The title has become more of a real honor over the years, but sometimes just bringing a convention to Louisville is good enough reason.

The image Kentuckians most like to project comes from the thousand square-mile patch of bluegrass in the middle of the state. The great farms like Calumet and Claiborne Stud, Spendthrift and Greentree and the horses they produce are the pride of a nation. Though it's strictly a rich man's game, and there are tobacco farmers in Kentucky who don't know where their next meal is coming from, horse-breeding is a passion shared by nearly everyone in the state. And why not? Nobody does it better.

Facing page: (top left) the Administration Building of the University of Louisville, (bottom left) Jefferson County Court House, and (top right) the Water Tower, all in Louisville. Bottom right: Heigold House, (left and below) the Brennan House, and (bottom) the mansion of Farmington, Louisville. Bottom left: the *Belle of Louisville*. Overleaf: (left) Founders Square, and (right) a clock in celebration of harness racing, Louisville.

Previous pages: the sternwheeler *Belle of Louisville*, on the Ohio River. Top and above: old-fashioned transport, and (left) an ornate house in Cherokee Park, Louisville. Facing page: (top) Louisville at night, and (bottom) Churchill Downs. Overleaf: (left) Monument to Zachary Taylor in the National Cemetery, Louisville, and (right) the Daniel Boone statue, Cherokee Park.

Facing page: an old, Jefferson County gristmill.
Top: the U.S. Gold Depository, Fort Knox. Above:
clapboard house outside Shelbyville, and (right)
a tobacco barn near Frankfort. Founded in 1786,
Frankfort was chosen as Kentucky's capital in
1792, and the present State Capitol (overleaf)
was built in 1910.

COMMONWEALTH of KENTUCKY
UNITED WE STAND
DIVIDED WE FALL

DANIEL BOONE'S GRAVE

BORN 1734; DIED 1820. ENTERED EASTERN
KENTUCKY, 1767; EXPLORED BLUEGRASS
REGION, 1769-71; GUIDED TRANSYLVANIA
COMPANY, BLAZED WILDERNESS TRAIL,
BUILT FORT BOONESBOROUGH IN 1775;
DIRECTED DEFENSE OF THE FORT, 1778;
EMIGRATED TO MISSOURI, 1799;
REINTERRED, WITH WIFE REBECCA, IN
FRANKFORT CEMETERY, 1845.
KENTUCKY DEPARTMENT OF HIGHWAYS

113

DANIEL BOONE

Previous pages: (left) Daniel Boone's grave, and (right) the statue of Abraham Lincoln in the rotunda of the State Capitol, Frankfort. Left: the clocktower of Paris City Hall, and (above) a church and barn east of Frankfort. Top and facing page: horses in the bluegrass country of the Lexington plain.

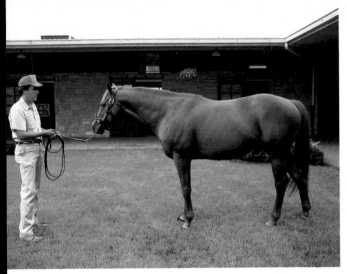

Previous pages: tobacco, growing (top right) west of Lexington, and drying (bottom right) in the field and (bottom left) gathered and hung in a barn. (Top left) barn east of Frankfort. The Bluegrass area of north central Kentucky is famed for the breeding of thoroughbred horses, such as those auctioned (facing page) at the Keeneland Horse Sale, and displayed (above) at Spendthrift's Stud Farm, Lexington. Top: the 1806 mansion of Ashland, at Lexington, home of the statesman Henry Clay. Right: the Memorial Hall of the University of Kentucky, Lexington.

Facing page: white-columned Waveland State
Shrine in Lexington, a Greek Revival mansion
built in 1847 by the grandson of Mary Boone, on
ground surveyed by Daniel Boone. Above:
bluegrass stables, and (top) Transylvania
University, Lexington. Right: the Shell Grotto
in Headley-Whitney Museum, Lexington.

Previous pages, this page and overleaf: trotting races at the Red Mile Harness Track in Lexington, known since 1875 as "the world's fastest harness track." Facing page: rodeo staged in the Rupp Arena in Lexington's Civic Center. Overleaf: (inset left) the Man O'War grave and memorial in Kentucky Horse Park, 1,032 acres of bluegrass dedicated to Kentucky's great tradition of horse breeding and racing. Other insets: bluegrass country.

Previous pages: Almahurst Farm, near Lexington.
Facing page: (top) White Hall, home of the 19th-century abolitionist Cassius Marcellus Clay, and (right) Madison County Courthouse, both in Richmond. Facing page: (bottom) the East Family Dwelling (1817), (top) the Center Family Dwelling (1824-34), and (above) smaller buildings, in the Shaker village of Pleasant Hill.

Berea College (above right), founded in 1855, is a vital, integral part of the town of Berea, in the foothills of the Cumberland Mountains. Above and facing page, top: Berea College Appalachian Museum, which depicts the traditions and culture of the southern Appalachians, and (top, and facing page, bottom) Churchill Weavers, a handweaving factory established in Berea in 1922. Right: the Boone Tavern Hotel, Berea.

SITE OF LOG COURTHOUSE
...
Kentucky District Court sessions held here March 14, 1785, until Court of Appeals set up in 1792. Created by Virginia statute on May 6, 1782, the court first met in Harrodsburg on March 3, 1783. Later meetings at Low Dutch Station and John Crow's Station before moved here. Samuel McDowell, John Floyd, George Muter, first judges; Walker Daniel, prosecutor; John May, clerk.

49

The government of Kentucky began in Danville in 1785, when the town became the first capital of the Kentucky District of Virginia. Kentucky's first courthouse square has been authentically reproduced in the center of Danville as the Constitution Square State Shrine, and includes a replica of the original log courthouse (top) and memorials (left and facing page bottom). Above: M. Lincoln House near Springfield, and (facing page, top) pastureland near Danville.

HERE
IN APRIL 1792
KENTUCKY'S FIRST CONSTITUTION
WAS FRAMED AND ADOPTED
AND
ANOTHER EMPIRE WAS BORN

Greek Revival-style pillars front Clay Hill (below), on Beaumont Avenue, Harrodsburg, and St. Joseph's Cathedral (bottom left), in Bardstown. Left: the Confederate Memorial near Perryville, and (bottom) the reproduction of Old Fort Harrod in Harrodsburg. Founded in 1774, this was the first permanent English settlement west of the Alleghenies. Facing page: (top) the "Old Kentucky Home" of Federal Hill, made famous by the composer Stephen Foster, and (bottom) the Wickland mansion, both in Bardstown.

Below: farmland near Smithland, and (right) St. Francis de Sales Church, Paducah. Bottom: the bronze Lincoln Statue in the public square of Hodgenville, and (bottom right) the Abraham Lincoln Birthplace Memorial, three miles south of Hodgenville, which houses the log cabin believed to have been the President's first home. Facing page: (top) sunset in industrial Henderson, and (bottom) John J. Audubon State Park, Henderson.

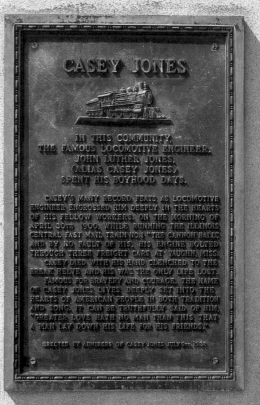

Facing page: (top) still water near Bandwell, (bottom) the prehistoric Wickliffe Mound Site, Wickliffe. Above: the strange parade of statues of the Wooldridge Monument in Mayfield, commissioned by Henry G. Wooldridge and carved before his death in 1899. Right: the Casey Jones Monument, Cayce, and (top) Lake Kentucky.

Barns, (top) near Lake Malone, and (above) near Hopkinsville. Left: Jefferson Davis Monument, Fairview. Facing page: (top left) fountain in Central Square, (top right) Felts Log House, (bottom left) a fine mansion, and (bottom right) Dr. Henry Hardin Cherry Hall at Western Kentucky University, all in Bowling Green.

Ruins of Karnak

Previous pages: (left) Ruins of Karnac, part of
the Mammoth Onyx Cave (right). Facing page:
(top) Old Mulkey Meeting House, Tompkinville,
and (bottom) replica of the first house in the
state, built in 1750 by Dr. Thomas Walker,
Barbourville. Top: Cumberland Falls, and (above)
the first Kentucky Fried Chicken Restaurant,
Corbin. Right: cornfield near Barbourville.

Left: bridge over the Cumberland River (top).
Above: Red River Gorge, where the river is crossed
by the Rock Bridge (facing page, top). Facing
page: (bottom) watermill on Levi Jackson
Wilderness Road, and (overleaf) the Appalachian
mountains seen from Kingdom Come State Park.

Facing page: (top) one of the twenty caves in Carter Caves State Resort Park near Olive Hill. (Bottom) industrial works at Ashland, and (top) the bridge linking Ashland with Ohio. Above: dilapidated barn, and (right) a farm track, south of Ashland.

Top: Bennets Mill Bridge, built in 1855 and
spanning Tygart's Creek, and (above)
Oldtown Bridge, built in 1880, near
Ashland. Right: a farm in wooded land near
Elliotsville, and (facing page) the
Kentucky Lock House. Overleaf left: (top)
the bridge from Maysville into Ohio.
(Bottom left) church spires in Maysville,
and (bottom right and right) the Church of
the Assumption, Covington. Following page:
reconstruction of an early Baptist church
outside Maysville.

EPHESUS   A D 431   DEFINES THE   BL VIRGIN   IS TRULY